LANDING YOUR TECH GIG IN 2024: A NOT-SO-SERIES GUIDE FOR SERIOUS ENGINEERS

Alan Hong

CONTENTS

Chapter 1: The Tech Landscape in 2024
Chapter 2: Crafting the Ultimate Engineer's Resume
Chapter 3: Networking Like a Pro (Even If You're an Introvert)
Chapter 4: Navigating the Job Application Process
Chapter 5: The Art of the Technical Interview
Chapter 6: Negotiating Your Salary Without Getting Ghosted
Chapter 7: Onboarding and Navigating Your First Job
Chapter 8: The Value of Learning Over Earning
Chapter 9: Remote Work and Industry Trends
Chapter 10: Keeping Your Sanity in the Code Jungle
Chapter 11: Startups vs. Corporations - Rethinking Stability in Tech
Chapter 12: Looking Ahead - Future-Proofing Your Tech Career

CHAPTER ONE
Chapter 1: The Tech Landscape in 2024

Chapter 1: The Tech Landscape in 2024

Welcome to the edge of tomorrow—or today? Time flies in the tech world, and keeping up can feel like you're strapped to a high-speed train, with landscapes changing more rapidly than fashion trends. And yes, I'm looking at you, neon leg warmers of the '80s.

AI: Your New Best Friend (Who's Also a Robot)

So, AI is everywhere. It's in your phone, your car, probably even deciding which socks you wear (if you've got those smart drawers, that is). But before you start picturing a future where AI steals your job and leaves you in the dust, let me offer a bit of reassurance: AI is more akin to the trusty hammer in your toolbox than the monster under your bed.

I get it, change can be as unsettling as finding out your quiet neighbor is a karaoke superstar. But here's the thing—we need not fear it. AI isn't out to replace us engineers; it's just another tool in our ever-expanding belt. Remember when the digital calculator debuted and threatened to end the reign of the slide-rule? (Ask your parents or grandparents what a slide-rule is). Spoiler alert: Engineers remained invaluable. It's the same drama, different era.

Engineers: Still the Cool Kids in Town

Amidst this AI extravaganza, we, the software engineers, still hold the key. We're behind the curtain, pulling the strings, teaching AI how to not just simulate life but enhance it under our guidance.

Our role is shifting, yes. But far from being demoted, we're now the directors of a grand play. Understanding AI, navigating its nuances, and, occasionally, gently correcting its attempts at making a cup of tea, are all in a day's work.

Regardless of where you stand on AI's encroachment into creative domains—be it writing, art, or music—the AI train is steaming ahead. It's better to be on it than watching it pass by.

Ready, Set, Adapt!

As a budding tech enthusiast in 2024, here's how you can skate through with style:

- **Stay Curious**: Tech is the wild west; exciting and unpredictable. Jump into AI, explore, and don't be scared to get a little digital dust on your boots.
- **Embrace Lifelong Learning**: Change is the only constant. Keep sharpening those skills, whether through online courses, bootcamps, or even the

odd enlightening TikTok.
- **Think Big, Think Ethical**: Crafting AI is more than a technical challenge; it's a moral one. Aim to build tech that betters the world, not just complicates it.
- **Be Like Water**: In the fluid world of tech, adaptability is your superpower. Yesterday's innovations are today's history. Keep learning, keep evolving, and you'll always be ahead.

Wrapping Up

Riding the waves of the tech landscape in 2024 doesn't have to be daunting. Remember, AI and new technologies are tools at our disposal, ready to be harnessed for creating a smarter, more connected world.

We're not just spectators in this technological evolution; we're at the helm. So, gear up with your coding skills, creative thinking, and maybe a good sense of humor. The future is ours to mold, one innovative line of code at a time.

CHAPTER TWO
Chapter 2: Crafting the Ultimate Engineer's Resume

Chapter 2: Crafting the Ultimate Engineer's Resume

So, you've decided to conquer the tech world, one job application at a time. Before you start envisioning your new desk with dual monitors and a mechanical keyboard that clicks just right, there's a dragon you need to slay first: your resume.

The Resume: Your Ticket to the Tech Kingdom

Think of your resume as the most important GitHub repository of your life, except instead of code, it's filled with your achievements, skills, and that one time you didn't burn down the house trying to build a Raspberry Pi home automation system.

The Basics: More Than Just Your Name and Address

Let's start with the basics. And no, I don't just mean

your name, contact info, and that awkwardly professional email address you created after realizing 'hotcoder69' might not make the best impression.
- **Headline & Summary**: Right off the bat, grab their attention with a headline that says more than just "aspiring software engineer." Think "Software Engineer with a Passion for Developing Scalable Web Applications and Eating Pizza." Then, a quick summary that tells your story better than your favorite streaming series. In two to three sentences, cover who you are, what you're amazing at, and what makes you leap out of bed at 3 PM.

Flaunt Your Projects: Show, Don't Tell

Projects are the heart and soul of your resume. They're your battle scars, your tales of glory. Don't just list them; flaunt them. For each project, include:
- **Title and Link**: Make sure the title is as captivating as a headline in a tech blog. And yes, include the link. If they can click it, they can't ignore it.
- **Technologies Used**: This isn't the time to be humble. Did you use React? Node.js? A mysterious framework only three people in the world know about? List them all.
- **Achievements**: Did your project increase user engagement, decrease loading times, or solve world hunger? Whatever the achievement, make it quantifiable and make it shine.

The Art of the Skill List: Be Specific

"Proficient in computer stuff" isn't going to cut it. Be specific. Break down your skills into categories like Programming Languages (Python, JavaScript), Frameworks (React, Django), Tools & Platforms (Git, AWS), and anything else relevant. Remember, this is like your tech wizard spell list—make it count.

Experience: It's Not Just About Jobs

No experience? No problem. Did you contribute to an open-source project, intern at a startup that paid you in experience (and maybe some coffee), or build something cool for your mom? That counts. Describe each role focusing on what you did, how you did it, and the impact it had. Use action verbs like "implemented," "developed," and "rescued" (for those particularly challenging bug fixes).

Tailoring Your Resume: An AI-Assisted Craft

Embrace the future by letting AI tools help tailor your resume. They're like a career coach that's always on, offering tips to match your resume to your dream job's description. Use these tools to optimize for keywords and personalize your resume for each application, but keep your unique voice front and center.

Embracing AI for the Win

Let AI be your ally in the resume game, guiding you to emphasize the skills and experiences that matter most. From suggesting the right keywords to helping with the layout, AI tools can ensure your resume stands out, but remember, it's your story they're telling.

Keeping It Authentic

While AI can give you an edge, your resume should still reflect who you are. Use AI suggestions as inspiration, not gospel. Your resume should be as unique as your code.

Your Resume, Your Story

Crafting your resume is like writing the first chapter of your next big adventure. It's about highlighting your past achievements, yes, but also about showcasing your potential. With a bit of creativity, strategic use of AI, and your unique flair, your resume will not just open doors—it'll break them down.

In the ever-evolving world of tech, your resume is your handshake, your first impression. Make it count, make it memorable, and let it reflect the incredible engineer you are set to become.

CHAPTER THREE

Chapter 3: Networking Like a Pro (Even If You're an Introvert)

Chapter 3: Networking Like a Pro (Even If You're an Introvert)

Welcome to the chapter that might initially make you a bit uneasy. But trust me, it's the kind of uneasy that leads to growth, opportunities, and perhaps a few new friends along the way. Yes, we're diving into networking—a concept that can evoke dread in even the most stalwart introvert.

Why Network?

In the rapidly spinning world of tech, it's not just what you know, but who knows you that can make all the difference. Networking opens doors to opportunities that you might never find on job boards: from insider industry knowledge, mentorship, collaborations, to the next step in your career. It's about weaving a web of connections that support your growth and where you can offer support in return.

Networking: Not Just for Extroverts

The mere mention of networking might conjure images of crowded conference rooms or awkward meet-and-greets. But let's set the record straight: networking isn't a one-size-fits-all endeavor, and it's definitely not reserved for the extroverts of the world.

Digital Platforms: Your Networking Allies

In 2024, your networking journey can flourish from the comfort of your keyboard. Here's where to plant those digital networking seeds:

- **LinkedIn**: The cornerstone of professional networking. Keep your profile polished, and don't hesitate to engage in discussions or share your achievements.
- **X (formerly Twitter)**: A bustling marketplace of ideas and insights where a simple reply or retweet can spark a meaningful connection.
- **GitHub**: Your code can do the talking. Contributing to projects and engaging with other developers can elevate your profile.
- **Meetup**: Whether you're looking for local coding clubs or virtual reality enthusiasts, Meetup connects you with like-minded tech aficionados.
- **Reddit**: Join targeted subreddits like r/programming to immerse yourself in the community, share knowledge, and seek advice.
- **Discord**: Tech-focused Discord servers are hubs of

real-time conversation and networking, often linked from other platforms like Reddit or X.

Crafting Your Elevator Pitch: A Real-World Example

Imagine being asked, "What do you do?" Here's a pitch that's brief yet impactful:

"I'm Jamie, a frontend developer specializing in creating accessible, user-friendly websites. Recently, I led the redesign of a nonprofit's site, boosting their engagement by 40%. I'm passionate about using tech to drive positive social change."

This pitch shares not just what you do, but how you make a difference—inviting further conversation.

The Value of In-Person Networking

While online networking is invaluable, there's something about face-to-face interactions that deepens connections. Use in-person events as a sandbox for your social skills:

- **Approach Them as Practice**: Each event is an opportunity to get comfortable with introducing yourself and articulating your passions and projects.
- **Quality Over Quantity**: Focus on having meaningful conversations, even if it's just with a few people, rather than trying to meet everyone in the room.

Why Network? For Growth and Opportunities

Networking, particularly for introverts, is less about forcing connections and more about finding your people, learning, and sharing. Both online platforms and in-person events offer fertile ground for planting the seeds of future opportunities. By stepping out of your comfort zone, you open the door to new paths in your tech career journey.

CHAPTER FOUR

Chapter 4: Navigating the Job Application Process

Chapter 4: Navigating the Job Application Process

Stepping into the job application arena with your resume in one hand and your cover letter in the other, it's time to make each application count. In 2024, where technology meets ambition, your approach needs to be as smart as it is enthusiastic.

Beyond Cold Applications: A Strategy for Success

Gone are the days of generic, one-size-fits-all applications. In an era where personalization is key, leveraging technology and insights can set you apart.

Tailoring with AI

Artificial intelligence isn't just transforming the way we work; it's also revolutionizing how we apply for work. AI tools can analyze job descriptions, suggesting tweaks to your resume and cover letter that align more closely with the employer's needs. This bespoke approach means your application speaks directly to what recruiters and hiring managers are looking for, making it more likely your resume will hit the mark.

Understanding the Role of Recruiters

Recruiters, whether third-party agents or in-house HR professionals, can be invaluable allies. But to work effectively with them, it's essential to know what they do (and don't) need from you.

Third-Party Recruiters

Think of third-party recruiters as your personal job market navigators. They're tuned into your needs and the market's demands. Transparent communication about your aspirations and deal-breakers helps them find the best fit for you.

In-House Recruiters

In-house recruiters are your direct line to the companies you're eager to join. They offer a window into the company culture and expectations. Interacting with them is your chance to make a memorable impression, so approach each conversation as you would an interview, armed with questions and a keen interest in the role.

Staying on the Recruiter's Radar

Persistence is key, but there's an art to following up. A thoughtful email or message reiterating your interest and asking for any updates shows you're proactive and genuinely interested, without being overbearing.

Considering Contract Roles: What You Need to

Know

As you navigate the tech job market, you'll likely come across contract roles. These positions, often project-based or for a fixed term, offer unique opportunities and flexibility but come with a different set of considerations compared to permanent roles.

- **Understanding Contract Roles**: Contract roles offer a chance to work on diverse projects, potentially with various companies, providing broad experience and a flexible work environment. They're particularly prevalent in the tech industry, where project needs can fluctuate rapidly.
- **Application Process**: When applying for contract roles, highlight your ability to quickly adapt to new environments and contribute immediately. Contractors are often expected to jump in with minimal onboarding, so showcasing your self-sufficiency and project-related achievements is key.
- **Higher Hourly Rates**: It's common for contract roles to offer higher hourly rates than salaried positions. This is in part because contractors have to manage their own taxes, health insurance, and other benefits, which are typically provided in permanent roles. The increased rate helps offset these additional responsibilities.
- **Managing Taxes and Insurance**: Contractors in the United States often work under a 1099 status, meaning they're responsible for their own taxes, including making quarterly estimated payments

to the IRS. This contrasts with W-2 employees, whose taxes are withheld by their employer. Understanding your tax obligations and planning for health insurance and retirement savings requires careful financial management.
- **No Standard Benefits**: Unlike permanent roles, contract positions rarely come with benefits like paid time off or health insurance. You'll need to plan for these expenses on your own, which can be a significant consideration when deciding between contract and permanent opportunities.
- **I-9 vs. W-2 Considerations**: Familiarize yourself with the I-9 form, used to verify employment eligibility in the United States for all employees, including contractors. Knowing whether you're being hired as a 1099 contractor or a W-2 employee through a contracting agency affects how your taxes are handled.
- **Negotiating Terms**: Because contract roles can vary widely in terms of compensation and conditions, negotiation is crucial. Discuss not just pay, but also project duration, expectations, and whether any benefits or resources (like equipment) are provided.
- **Varied Experiences and Transitioning to Permanent**: Contract roles can serve as a gateway to permanent positions, offering a way to demonstrate your value to a company. Excelling in a contract role can open doors to more long-term opportunities, making them a worthwhile option

for those looking to break into a particular sector or company.

Scam Awareness: Know What's Legit

In the digital age, scams are an unfortunate reality of the job search. Here's what legitimate recruiters will typically ask for:
- **Full Name**: To address you correctly and verify your application.
- **City and State/Province**: For location-specific opportunities or to understand time zone differences.
- **Citizenship or Visa Status**: Essential for understanding your eligibility to work in the country.

Anything beyond these basics, especially requests for sensitive personal information early in the process, is a red flag. Legitimate background checks and further details come later, often through formal channels, once a job offer is in serious consideration.

Adapting Your Approach for International Applications

When eyeing opportunities across borders, the intricacies of each country's job market come into play. From understanding local employment laws to recognizing customary application formats, adapting your approach can significantly boost your prospects. Here's what to keep in mind:
- **Research Local Norms**: Each country has its own nuances in the job application process, from the

expected resume length to the inclusion of personal details.
- **Cultural Sensitivity**: Be mindful of cultural differences, especially in communication styles, when engaging with international recruiters or companies.
- **Legal Requirements**: Familiarize yourself with visa requirements and work authorization processes to ensure you're a viable candidate from the get-go.

By tailoring your applications to respect and reflect the expectations of the international job markets you're interested in, you position yourself as a well-informed, adaptable candidate ready to take on global challenges.

Mastering the Application Process

The job application process in 2024 is both a science and an art, blending technology with personal touch. By smartly tailoring your applications with AI, maintaining open lines of communication with recruiters, and staying vigilant against scams, you're setting yourself up for success. Each application is a step towards your next big opportunity in the tech world.

CHAPTER FIVE

Chapter 5: The Art of the Technical Interview

Chapter 5: The Art of the Technical Interview

You've charmed them with your resume, dazzled them with your networking skills, and now it's time for the main event: the technical interview. Think of it as your first date with the company—except you're solving algorithms instead of sharing appetizers.

Understanding the Technical Interview

Imagine if solving puzzles and talking about your favorite projects could land you a job. Welcome to the technical interview, where this dream becomes reality—kind of.

- **The Format**: These interviews can feel like a pop quiz from every tech class you've ever taken, combined. One minute you're discussing the finer points of a binary search tree, the next you're solving a logic puzzle that feels like it came from a game show.

Preparation: Your Secret Weapon

Diving into a technical interview without preparation is like going to a sword fight armed with a spoon. You might make a point, but it won't be the one you intended.

- **Brush Up on Fundamentals**: Revisit those dusty textbooks or online tutorials. It's like revisiting old friends, except these friends ask you tough questions about data structures and algorithms.
- **Practice Coding Out Loud**: It's a bit like explaining a recipe while cooking, but instead of a delicious meal, you end up with a beautifully optimized piece of code. Get comfortable articulating your thought process; it's a skill that turns good candidates into great ones.
- **Mock Interviews**: Like rehearsal dinner before the big day, except you're rehearsing for your dream job. Use peers or online platforms to simulate the interview experience and get feedback. Remember, practice makes permanent!

During the Interview: Showtime

Now's your chance to shine brighter than a well-commented block of code.

- **Think Aloud**: Treat your interviewer like a rubber duck. Explain your thought process as if they're there to help debug your brain. It's less about finding the perfect solution and more about

showing how you tackle problems.
- **Ask Clarifying Questions**: Asking questions doesn't show weakness; it shows you're methodical. Plus, it buys you time to think, and who doesn't need more of that?
- **Admit What You Don't Know**: It's like acknowledging you haven't seen every episode of "Star Trek." Embarrassing, but honest. Better to admit a gap in your knowledge than to boldly go into the realm of making things up.

Tackling Coding Challenges

Here, you're not just writing code; you're writing your ticket to a job offer.
- **Read and Clarify**: Misunderstanding the problem is like starting a road trip without knowing the destination. Sure, you'll end up somewhere interesting, but it might not be where you wanted.
- **Start with a Brute Force Solution**: If you can't see the forest for the trees, at least start chopping down a tree. Any solution is better than staring blankly at the interviewer.
- **Optimize**: Once you've got something that works, it's time to make it work better. Think of it as streamlining your code the way you'd streamline your morning coffee routine—efficiently and with style.

Post-Interview: The Reflective Comedian

Reflect on your performance like you're reviewing a stand-up set. What got laughs (or nods), and what bombed? Send a follow-up that shows you're interested and gives a callback to a highlight of the interview, making you memorable for all the right reasons.

Embrace the Challenge

Technical interviews are your chance to be the hero in your own tech saga. Each one is a learning experience, a chance to get better, and occasionally, a source of funny stories. Remember, even if you stumble, it's just part of the journey. The right role is out there, and each interview is a step closer to finding it.

CHAPTER SIX

Chapter 6: Negotiating Your Salary Without Getting Ghosted

Chapter 6: Negotiating Your Salary Without Getting Ghosted

Navigating salary negotiations is like the boss level in your favorite game—challenging but immensely rewarding when done right. It's your chance to ensure the compensation reflects your worth and sets you up for success.

Know Your Worth (Then Add Tax)

Start with research. Tools like Glassdoor, PayScale, LinkedIn Salary, and Levels.fyi are your best friends, providing a landscape of what's fair and expected. It's like setting your GPS before you start driving—you need to know where you're going.

The Opening Offer: The Beginning, Not the End

That initial offer is just the start. It's tempting to say

yes right away, especially when it's your first big job offer. However, taking a moment to breathe and assess the offer fully can make a significant difference in the long run.

- **Pause for Effect**: Acknowledge the offer and express your excitement, but ask for time to review it thoroughly. This isn't about playing games; it's about making informed decisions.

Consider the Whole Package: Growth Over Gold

When you're new to the field, the salary figure might catch your eye first, but there's more to a job than its paycheck.

- **Value Learning and Growth**: Positions that offer extensive learning opportunities often outweigh the ones with a slightly higher starting salary. A role that challenges you, exposes you to new technologies, and offers mentorship can be far more beneficial in building a solid foundation for your career.
- **Long-Term Vision**: Think about where a job can take you. Early career choices can significantly influence your career path, so opting for roles that promise comprehensive growth and learning can lead to greater rewards down the line.

Crafting Your Counteroffer: The Gentle Art of Persuasion

Your counteroffer should be like a well-crafted argument in a friendly debate—clear, concise, and backed by evidence.

- **Be Precise and Reasoned**: Use your research to justify your counteroffer. It's not about demanding more; it's about demonstrating your value and finding a mutually agreeable number.
- **Stay Open**: Indicate your flexibility. Negotiation is a two-way street, and showing that you're open to discussion fosters goodwill and a positive start to your potential relationship with the employer.

Juggling Multiple Offers: A Balancing Act

Having multiple offers is like having several good cards in your hand—you want to play them wisely.

- **Use Offers Strategically**: Letting companies know you have other options can sometimes lead to better offers, but always be tactful and honest in your communications.

Accepting an Offer: The Strategic Yes

In the challenging job market of 2024, especially for new grads, experience is gold. If an offer doesn't tick every box but promises solid growth and learning opportunities, consider accepting it. Every role is a stepping stone to the next, often with unexpected opportunities for advancement and skill development.

Your Career, Your Terms

Salary negotiations mark a pivotal point in your job search journey. They're not just about securing a job but about affirming your value in the tech industry. While the immediate goal might be to land a position, the broader aim is to advance in a career that's rewarding both professionally and personally.

Remember, the choices you make early on can set the direction for your future path, so choose wisely, with an eye on both the present and the horizon.

CHAPTER SEVEN

Chapter 7: Onboarding and Navigating Your First Job

Chapter 7: Onboarding and Navigating Your First Job

Congratulations are in order—you've landed the job! But as you step into this new role, remember, it's about laying the foundations for your career while ensuring you maintain a healthy balance between work and life.

The Onboarding Process: Your Gateway

Onboarding is your official welcome wagon, but it's also your first taste of the company's culture and expectations. Dive in, ask questions, and start as you mean to go on—eager to learn and ready to contribute.

Mastering Your Role: Setting the Stage for Success

Define what success looks like with your manager early on. Clear goals not only provide direction but also ensure you're aligned with your team's and company's objectives. Be proactive in your learning and seek opportunities to add value.

Building Relationships: The Network Effect

The connections you forge now can influence your career trajectory in profound ways. Look for mentors and collaborators among your new colleagues. These relationships can offer guidance, support, and even opportunities in the future. Remember, networking doesn't stop once you've landed the job; it's an ongoing process.

Work-Life Balance: Drawing Boundaries

Maintaining a healthy work-life balance is crucial, not just for your well-being but for your long-term career health. It's perfectly acceptable to log off at 5 pm and mute work notifications after hours. If you find yourself in a culture that demands constant availability, assess whether this aligns with your values and long-term goals. Remember, your worth is not defined by your productivity alone.

- **Setting Boundaries**: It's important to establish healthy boundaries from the outset. Clearly communicate your working hours and be consistent in respecting your off-time.
- **Finding Flexibility**: Flexibility can be key, especially in demanding projects. However, it should never come at the expense of your health or personal time. Strive for a balance that allows you to be productive at work and fulfilled in your personal life.

Navigating Challenges: The Art of Perseverance

Mistakes are inevitable, but they're also invaluable learning opportunities. Embrace challenges as chances to grow, and don't shy away from seeking feedback. It's through these experiences that you'll find areas for personal and professional development.

Continuous Improvement: Never Stop Learning

The tech landscape is always evolving, and so should you. Stay curious, keep learning, and remain open to new experiences within your role and the broader tech community.

Loyalty vs. Career Growth: Making Informed Choices

Understand that in the business world, the exchange of services for compensation is the core of your employment relationship. Loyalty to a company should never come at the cost of your personal growth or well-being. If a role doesn't meet your needs or align with your values, it's okay to continue your job search until you find the right fit.

Your Career, Your Journey

Your first job is just the beginning of a long and exciting career journey. By actively engaging in the onboarding process, setting clear goals, building strong professional relationships, maintaining a healthy work-life balance, and staying open to continuous learning, you're not just succeeding in your current role. You're building a foundation for a fulfilling career in tech. Keep networking, keep learning, and remember—the tech community is vast yet interconnected. The relationships you build today may open doors you never imagined tomorrow.

CHAPTER EIGHT

Chapter 8: The Value of Learning Over Earning

Chapter 8: The Value of Learning Over Earning

Embarking on your tech career is akin to setting sail in uncharted waters. While the temptation of high salaries might beckon like sirens, it's the pursuit of knowledge and diverse experiences that charts the course to true fulfillment and success.

Embracing the Learning Journey

Your early career decisions have a profound impact, not just on your immediate job satisfaction but on your long-term growth and versatility in the tech industry. Understanding the spectrum from junior to senior roles is crucial, but so is recognizing the value in the vast array of tech-adjacent positions available to you.

- **Junior to Senior Evolution**: Progressing in your career involves deepening your technical expertise

and also honing your ability to mentor, communicate, and lead. Seniority in tech is marked not just by what you know, but by how effectively you can share that knowledge and inspire innovation in others.
- **The Rich Tapestry of Tech-Adjacent Roles**: Exploring roles like Solutions Engineer, QA Engineer, DevOps, or Product Manager can open new avenues for learning. These positions often require a blend of technical knowledge and soft skills, such as strategic thinking and communication, broadening your professional skill set.

The Compound Interest of Continuous Learning

Investing in roles that challenge you and offer opportunities for growth pays dividends in the form of enhanced skills, knowledge, and professional satisfaction. Each new experience builds upon the last, creating a rich foundation for a dynamic and resilient career.
- **Broadening Your Horizon**: Whether through lateral moves or stepping into entirely new domains within tech, embracing a variety of roles throughout your career can make you more adaptable and invaluable in the fast-evolving tech landscape.
- **Prioritizing Growth Over Immediate Gain**: Sometimes, the best career moves aren't the ones that offer the highest salary upfront but those that promise the most enriching experiences. Look for

roles that will push you out of your comfort zone and offer the greatest potential for learning.

Navigating Career Transitions

As you consider transitions, whether advancing from junior to mid-level, stepping into a senior role, or exploring tech-adjacent fields, focus on the opportunities each change presents for personal and professional development.

- **Evaluating Opportunities for Learning**: Assess potential roles not just by the immediate benefits they offer but by their capacity to expand your expertise, expose you to new challenges, and enhance your problem-solving and leadership abilities.
- **Leveraging Overlapping Skills**: Recognize the skills that are transferable across different roles and how they can position you for success in various areas of the tech industry. The analytical mindset of a developer, the process orientation of a QA Engineer, and the strategic vision of a Product Manager are assets in virtually any tech-related role.

Charting Your Unique Path

The tech industry offers a labyrinth of pathways, each leading to its own set of challenges and rewards. By prioritizing opportunities that offer the deepest learning experiences and embracing the journey through different roles and responsibilities, you're not just building a career; you're cultivating a continuously evolving repertoire of skills and insights. Remember, in the vast and varied landscape of technology, your growth and learning are the true measures of your success.

CHAPTER NINE

Chapter 9: Remote Work and Industry Trends

Chapter 9: Remote Work and Industry Trends

As the tech world embraces remote work like a coder hugs their coffee mug, we find ourselves redefining what it means to be "at work." Here's how to not just survive but thrive in the remote work era, all while keeping your sanity and sense of humor intact.

Embracing the Remote Work Revolution

Adapting to remote work isn't just about changing your location; it's about changing your mindset. And sometimes, it's about convincing your pet that your keyboard is not a bed.

Creating an Effective Workspace: Your mission, should you choose to accept it, is to create a workspace that's more conducive to coding than couch-potatoing. It's about finding that sweet spot where you're not tempted to nap every hour.

Maintaining Discipline and Structure: Establish a routine that clearly differentiates between work time and me-time. Remember, working from home means you're always at the office, but it shouldn't always feel that way. Transitioning from your work zone to your chill zone can be as simple as closing a door or just stepping away from the desk and doing your best "I'm done for the day" dance.

Investing in Quality Equipment: If your company offers a stipend, use it to spruce up your home office. A high-quality microphone and webcam can elevate your Zoom presence from "witness protection program" to "prime-time news anchor." And let's not forget, upgrading your home internet not only smooths out work calls but also drastically reduces the chances of rage-quitting your after-hours gaming session due to lag.

Staying Connected in a Remote World

In the remote work era, staying connected means more than just endless video calls that could have been emails.

Regular Check-Ins and Virtual Team Building: Engage in virtual team activities that don't always revolve around work. Whether it's an online escape room or a virtual coffee break, these moments can add a dash of social spice to your work routine, reminding you that your teammates are more than just talking heads on your screen.

Keeping Pace with Industry Trends

The tech industry waits for no one, and staying updated is your ticket to remaining relevant (and employable).

Continuous Learning and Networking: Carve out time to learn the latest in tech, but remember, it's okay to unplug. After all, the best ideas often strike when you're not staring at a screen. As for networking, remember that today's awkward Zoom mixer could be where you meet your future co-founder or boss.

Navigating Career Growth Remotely

Growing your career remotely means making sure your hard work is seen, not just felt.

Showcasing Your Achievements: In the world of remote work, out of sight should not mean out of mind. Make your accomplishments known, because your cat's admiration, while heartwarming, won't get you that promotion.

Remote Work, the Final Frontier

Remote work is here to stay, and mastering it is like leveling up in the most complex game you've ever played. But with the right setup, attitude, and internet speed, you're not just surviving; you're thriving. Welcome to the future of work, where every day is casual Friday, and the commute is as short as the walk from your bed to your desk.

CHAPTER TEN

Chapter 10: Keeping Your Sanity in the Code Jungle

Chapter 10: Keeping Your Sanity in the Code Jungle

In the grand coding saga of your life, where you battle bugs by day and dream in JavaScript by night, it's crucial to remember: even the most hardcore developers need a break. Here's how to keep your mind sharp and your spirits high, without turning into a walking (or sitting) stereotype of the overworked tech enthusiast.

Recognizing the Signs: More Human, Less Cyborg

If you've started giving real-life objects variable names or see matrix codes when you close your eyes, it might be time to hit the pause button. Your brain isn't just for storing programming languages; it needs some downtime too.

- **Listen to Your Body and Mind**: If you're guzzling

coffee like water and your most meaningful conversations are with your rubber duck debugger, it's a sign to reassess your work-life blend.

Setting Boundaries: The Noble Art of "Nope"

In a world that idolizes the "always-on" mode, learning to power down is your superpower.

- **Guard Your Time Like a Dragon Hoards Gold**: It's okay to say no to back-to-back Zoom calls or to projects that eat into your me-time. Your calendar isn't a challenge to see how much you can fit into one day.
- **Shutdown Rituals**: Cultivate an end-of-day ritual that signals your brain it's time to log off. Whether it's a literal shutting down of your computer or a victory lap around the living room, make it yours.

Mental Health in the Digital Realm: An Epic Quest for Balance

Your online life is vibrant, but it shouldn't be the only life you lead. Finding balance in the digital age is like finding the perfect coffee-to-code ratio.

- **Embrace the Digital Detox**: Occasionally, unplug from all things electronic. Your emails can wait. Yes, even that one. Your mind will thank you, and your gaming skills won't suffer—promise.
- **Build a Fellowship**: Surround yourself with people who can laugh with you about the absurdities of tech life but also remind you there's a world outside GitHub.

Self-Care: Not Just for NPCs

Treating yourself as the main character means more than just surviving; it means thriving beyond the code.

- **Get Physical**: Move your body in ways that make you happy. Dance like nobody's watching, or at least like your webcam is off.
- **Cultivate Offline Joy**: Rediscover hobbies that don't involve a screen. Painting, cooking, rock climbing—activities that remind you life is beautifully high-res, with no loading times.

The Ultimate Cheat Code

Balancing mental health and work in the tech world doesn't come with a one-size-fits-all solution. It's about finding what works for you, making adjustments as you go, and remembering to laugh at the absurdity of it all. Your career is important, but it's just one part of your epic quest. After all, even the most dedicated coder needs to log off and recharge, lest you start dreaming in binary. Remember, in the grand game of life, ensuring you're happy and healthy is the ultimate win.

CHAPTER ELEVEN

Chapter 11: Startups vs. Corporations - Rethinking Stability in Tech

Chapter 11: Startups vs. Corporations - Rethinking Stability in Tech

In your tech career journey, the decision between diving into the vibrant startup scene or navigating the structured pathways of corporate giants isn't just about choosing where to work. It's about defining what stability means to you and how you build it through your experiences, growth, and adaptability in an industry known for its rapid evolution.

Redefining Stability: The Startup Perspective

In the startup world, stability doesn't come from staying still. It's the agility to adapt, the breadth of experience you gain, and the versatility of your skill set that form your career's bedrock.

- **Pros**: The startup environment is a dynamic

classroom, offering lessons in cutting-edge technology, project leadership, and innovation daily. Each role is an opportunity to add new tools to your arsenal, making you a highly sought-after tech professional.
- **A Different Kind of Stability**: Viewing startups as less stable overlooks the personal growth and resilience built through navigating their challenges. This journey crafts a tech warrior, ready for whatever the industry throws their way.

The Corporate Empire: A Different Battlefield

Corporations offer a contrasting landscape of opportunities and challenges, where stability might seem more traditional but comes with its own set of demands for adaptability and growth.
- **Pros**: With vast resources and structured environments, corporations can offer a steady climb up the career ladder, access to in-depth training in your field, and the security of well-established processes and benefits.
- **Navigating the Terrain**: Corporations, too, face their cycles of change. Staying adaptable, seeking continuous learning opportunities, and not shying away from internal mobility can help you maintain relevancy and drive in these settings.

Choosing Your Path: Valuing Experience Over Predictability

Deciding where your loyalties lie requires a deep dive into what you value more: the thrill of varied experiences and rapid growth in startups or the depth of specialization and structured progression in corporations.

- **For the Agile Adventurers**: If a high-paced, ever-changing environment sounds like your kind of quest, the startup landscape beckons. Here, your stability is measured by your ability to thrive in diverse settings.
- **For the Calculated Strategists**: Those drawn to specialization, structure, and comprehensive planning might find their place in the corporate world. Yet, the true measure of success lies in seeking challenges and broadening your skill set within these environments.

Crafting Your Unique Definition of Stability

Stability in the tech world transcends the traditional notions tied to the size or age of a company. It's found in the richness of your experiences, your commitment to lifelong learning, and your ability to navigate change. Whether through startups or corporations, building a career that reflects your values, leverages your strengths, and satisfies your quest for growth is the ultimate achievement in tech.

CHAPTER TWELVE

Chapter 12: Looking Ahead - Future-Proofing Your Tech Career

Chapter 12: Looking Ahead - Future-Proofing Your Tech Career

As we approach the end of our digital odyssey, it's clear that the tech landscape is more like quicksand than solid ground—constantly shifting under our feet. But fear not! The future is bright for those who are ready to ride the waves of change rather than get swept away. Let's explore how to not just survive but thrive in the future of tech.

Embracing the Constant of Change

The first step in future-proofing your career is to accept that change is the only constant. Like trying to predict the next big thing in tech, it's a bit of a guessing game, but with better odds if you keep your skills sharp and your mind open.

- **Stay Curious**: Curiosity didn't kill the cat; it made it a tech mogul. Foster a mindset of lifelong learning, always exploring new technologies, methodologies, and industry trends.
- **Adaptability is Key**: Like a chameleon in a disco, the ability to adapt to new environments and challenges will make you stand out. Flexibility in your skills and approach to work can open doors you didn't even know existed.

Building a Diverse Skill Set

In a world where today's cutting-edge is tomorrow's old news, having a toolbox filled with a variety of skills is your ticket to longevity in the tech industry.

- **Go Beyond Coding**: Understanding the business, mastering soft skills like communication and teamwork, and getting comfortable with project management can make you invaluable, no matter where the tech tide turns.
- **Embrace Cross-Disciplinary Learning**: The future belongs to those who can find the intersections between tech and other fields—be it AI and healthcare, blockchain and finance, or IoT and sustainability. The more dots you can connect, the more opportunities you'll find.

Networking and Community Engagement

Building a network is like planting a garden; it requires time and care but grows into something that can support and nourish you throughout your career.

- **Stay Engaged with the Tech Community**: Attend

conferences (virtual or in-person), participate in hackathons, and contribute to open-source projects. These activities not only bolster your resume but also keep you connected to the heartbeat of the industry.
- **Mentorship Matters**: Be a mentor and find a mentor. Sharing knowledge and experience not only helps others grow but also reinforces your understanding and opens up new perspectives on your own career path.

Preparing for the Future

As we stand on the brink of new technological frontiers, from quantum computing to augmented reality and beyond, the possibilities are as limitless as your willingness to explore them.
- **Think Big, Start Small**: You don't have to master everything at once. Pick one area of emerging technology that intrigues you and start learning. Small steps can lead to giant leaps in your career.
- **Flexibility Over Planning**: While it's great to have a plan, be prepared to pivot. The tech industry's next big thing might be something no one has even thought of yet. Stay flexible in your goals and open to unexpected opportunities.

The Adventure Continues

As we close this guide, remember that your tech career is an ongoing adventure—one filled with challenges, triumphs, and continual learning. The future is unwritten, offering a canvas on which you can paint your unique path. Keep learning, stay adaptable, and above all, enjoy the journey. After all, in the tech industry, the next chapter is always just a startup, an innovation, or an idea away.

Made in the USA
Columbia, SC
08 October 2024

43954982R00028